RULES
AND
CONSEQUENCES

RULES
AND
CONSEQUENCES

One Major Reason Why They Don't Always Work and What Else Teachers Can Do

Regenia Mitchum Rawlinson

Village Concepts Consultants, LLC

Published by Village Concepts Consultants, LLC

ISBN: 978-1-5480-2313-3

Typesetting services by BOOKOW.COM

Gratitude to my husband David, who is my best friend and strongest advocate, and to my children, David II, Bradford, and Brittany, who taught me more about myself than I thought I needed to learn.

PREFACE

James, a fifteen-year-old high school student, was expelled for threatening and yelling at his teacher. Since he was classified as learning disabled, federal law mandated that the school provide a certified teacher to teach him at home. I agreed to be James's homebound instructor for five hours each week for a total of 155 hours. The principal agreed to James earning two credits if he finished his homebound hours and completed all assignments with 70 percent accuracy.

James came to the first five sessions. He was too young to drive, so he walked to and from the public library where we agreed to meet. Our session did not end until well after dark. I asked him if his mother would be picking him up, and he said that she had to be places and would not have time to come for him after tutoring. I called his mother to discuss this with her. She promised to come, but each time he ended up walking the three miles to his house in the dark. I wanted to take him home, but it was against school policy to do so.

One night there was a downpour and a brisk wind. I could not reach his mother, and James had no choice but to walk. I waited with James until the rain slowed to a drizzle, and I could only hope he would reach home before it started raining heavily again.

James skipped the sixth and seventh meetings. I called his mother to inquire about him. She told me he had not been home for the last few days, and she did not know where he was. When he showed up for the eighth session, I asked him to explain his absences. He refused to discuss it and was distant and uncooperative for the entire session.

I had recently completed training on the activity of different gangs. It was obvious that James was involved with a gang based on his clothing and markings on his book bag. I questioned him about them, and he denied being involved with a gang. I did not say anything else about gangs to him that afternoon, thinking I would discuss the subject with his mother later.

When I called his mother to discuss his behavior and the gang markings on his bag, she informed me that she knew he was in a gang, but she could do nothing about it. She lamented about James being arrested several times for drug possession and theft.

She said, "I have my own life to live, and James is messing things up for me. I gave up on him because he is nothing but trouble and I don't have time to mess with him anymore."

I asked how long she had suspected that James was involved in a gang. She responded, "James stayed with my sister in another state since he was five years old until last year when he turned fourteen. My sister could not keep him anymore because of her health. I had to work and could not be with him twenty-four hours a day. One day I came home, and he had a tattoo on his arm. He has been in and out of trouble since that day."

James did not return to tutoring after the eighth meeting. I learned a few weeks later that he had been arrested for drug possession. His homebound instruction had been rescinded. James was already on probation and this meant he would be detained in a juvenile facility for several years.

What happened to James? Did he feel rejected by his mother, then his aunt, and then his mother again? What about his father? What about school? Did he feel like he belonged, or did he meet with more rejection? Was James angry with his mother and brought that anger to school? These and many questions come to mind when I think about James. The question that I grapple with the most is what did James require that he did not get from home or school? Could more have been done for James at school and in the classroom? What would have made things different for James?

Many children come to school with unfulfilled needs. Frustrated when their desires such as care, acceptance, appreciation, love, belonging, and warmth are ignored, some of these children behave in unacceptable ways in school. The question educators must answer is, how can they provide for some of these needs in school and the classroom? RULES and CONSEQUENCES: One Major Reason Why They Don't Always Work and What Else Teachers Can Do is an attempt to answer this question.

Acknowledgments

I would like to acknowledge my parents, Solomon (deceased) and Hazel Mitchum for their commitment to education.

"Perception is so powerful that it can make you deny reality."

CONTENTS

THE CHALLENGE

IN 1975, the year I started teaching at an elementary school, educators in my school identified discipline as a serious issue. Thirty years later, I am a high school counselor, and discipline remains a top concern for educators. When I listen to news reports, I hear educators from around the country voicing the same concerns about discipline as educators at my school and identifying discipline as a priority. Many schools list gang activity, fighting, assault, and disrespect to staff as regular occurrences. Students are frequently arrested at school for bringing weapons and disturbing the peace.

My review of hundreds of discipline referrals at my school and in my district verified that discipline problems continue to present a challenge for educators. The national newspapers detail accounts of the same issues happening in schools throughout the country. Columbine, where two students killed twelve students, one teacher, and injured twenty-four others before taking their own lives, is a chilling reminder of discipline issues educators face in the schools.

Bullying has become a serious problem in schools, including my own. Students complain to me and other counselors and administrators weekly about being pushed, threatened, called names, assaulted, and intimidated. According to the students, these disturbing accounts of bullying happen in the cafeteria, bathrooms, classrooms, and hallways. Many students are afraid to be alone at school. Some students move around in groups for their protection. Teachers and administrators have less time to devote to improving math skills or increasing reading levels when they must take time to discipline students who bully fellow schoolmates.

At our regular staff meetings, teachers frequently discuss how frustrating it is for them to spend time disciplining students for excessive talking, acting disrespectful, and refusing to follow directions. The teachers voice concern about students' lack of achievement because time on task is reduced when teachers must devote an inordinate amount of time to correcting students. When instructional time is lost, students are in jeopardy of failing to meet standards on high-stakes testing. Teachers report that they address a variety of behaviors on a regular basis to include: 1) inappropriate talking, 2) disrespect of other students, 3) throwing paper, 4) unauthorized use of cell phones, 5) refusal to follow directions, 6) talking back, 7) arguing with peers and teachers, and 8) getting out of seats.

It is concerning that educators have not found a way to reduce incidences of unacceptable behaviors. If discipline problems are a looming threat to the well-being of students and educators, how are educators being prepared to effectively address discipline issues?

When I was earning my degrees in education, the required courses scarcely addressed classroom discipline. On the rare occasion when classroom discipline was addressed, the focus was on establishing rules and consequences. A critique of these courses led me to the conclusion that rules, and consequences were the only aspects of discipline educators were concerned with. The premise of these courses seems to have been that to address discipline, one merely needed to establish a set of rules and consequences. I have begun to question this narrow view of discipline.

Over the course of my teaching career, I have observed classrooms in numerous schools to critique behavioral strategies and provide feedback to teachers for improvement. During these visits, I found most, if not all, classrooms had a list of rules and consequences posted on the wall. If rules and consequences could reduce discipline problems, there would have been fewer discipline problems in most of the classrooms.

The reality is that rules and consequences as a discipline plan have yielded disappointing results. I conducted an informal Internet survey of teachers in my state. I asked them how often instruction was interrupted because they had to stop and address student misconduct. Teachers were asked to respond by selecting daily, weekly, monthly, or rarely. Five hundred and forty (540) teachers responded. Over four hundred and eighty (480) teachers, or 90 percent, responded "daily." The remaining fifty-four teachers said "weekly" or "monthly." My second question was, "Do you have rules and consequences posted in your classroom?" Five hundred and thirty-five responded "yes." This survey suggests addressing discipline issues requires much of teachers' time and attention.

I have concluded that there must be more to discipline than rules and consequences. Students must feel like they belong, have bonds with others, are accepted, reassured, appreciated, and valued to reduce the frequency of misconduct.

I contemplated why students were behaving inappropriately. Teachers made the following assertions in a second survey that asked, why do you think students misbehave? Most of the teachers responded with students are lazy, do not care, are unmotivated, lack self-discipline, do not respect authority, and lack parental involvement.

These responses from teachers prompted an additional question: Who did teachers believe was responsible for changing student behavior, themselves, students, parents, or administrators? I asked sixty randomly selected teachers at my school and many said the students, parents, and administrators were accountable for ensuring students behaved appropriately. I surmised from the answer to this question that teachers felt they were less responsible for changing student behavior than others.

Historically, teachers looked to parents and administrators for help with reducing discipline problems. Parents and administrators typically spanked and scolded children and took away privileges. Administrators might suspend the students, remove them from the classroom, call parents, or give detention. Depending on parents and administrators to address discipline often initiates a "pass the buck" scenario: teachers refer students to administrators, administrators call home, parents call teachers, and the cycle continues.

Perhaps changing how educators think about discipline could alter their approach to it. The historical approach to discipline problems has not worked. A new approach is needed. In this book, I have drawn on my decades of experience as an educator to develop a new approach to education, one that focuses on the needs of children. For many educators, this would be a paradigm shift.

More than Rules and Consequences

Mrs. Smith teaches a seventh-grade class of students with several different personalities. Brooks was often sent to the principal to be disciplined because he told jokes and laughed incessantly. Melissa had to be removed from group activities several times because she would monopolize the conversation and become angry when she did not get her way. Samuel greeted everyone each day with a hug. Don would study long hours for a test because it was important to him to make the highest grade. Susan did not complete assignments because she did not see the relevance of education to her life. Rodney joined a street gang because he did not have many friends at school. What can Mrs. Smith do to accommodate Brooks' need for fun, Melissa's need for power, Samuel's need for love, Don's need for respect and affirmation, Susan's need for support, and Rodney's need for protection, acceptance, and alliance? *RULES and CONSEQUENCES: One Major Reason Why They Don't Always Work and What Else Teachers Can Do* will provide some answers to this question.

It has been my experience that meeting the needs of students is one of the keys to changing student behavior. I asked myself what approach would be effective in meeting the needs of students to decrease discipline problems. As I thought about developing an approach, I decided to focus on two tasks. The first task was to find commonalities among love, acceptance, alliance, respect, appreciation, support, protection, shelter, and affirmation and categorize them. I decided that love, acceptance, and respect were about making connections. Protection, shelter, and alliance point to security. Affirmation and appreciation imply reward. Support indicates a need for a variety of services and I will call this category "support services".

Connection is about building relationships between students and teachers to enhance the learning environment. Reward discusses recognition and appreciation of students. Security addresses providing a safe, secure, and warm environment for students. Support services provide a network of support to include classroom beliefs and goal setting. The desire for connection, reward, security, and support services can unfold individually or collectively. When students feel connected, rewarded, secure, and supported, they will alter their behavior for the better.

I have had the opportunity to observe many educators and work in many schools as a teacher, consultant, and school counselor. I have found that educators understand the desire for students to feel connected, rewarded, secure, and supported. Educators know that satisfying students will improve their behavior. But attempts by educators to provide students with what they need produced less than positive results. This prompted two questions: Could the needs of the students be provided for in a systematic manner? And what would happen if these needs were addressed in a systematic manner in the classroom? I decided that the answer to the first question was "yes" and I believed that students would respond positively with decreased misbehaviors to such a methodical addressing of their needs.

My second task was to develop a framework that could be implemented in the classroom. I reflected on my experiences as a teacher and classroom disciplinarian. I compared my role as a teacher to that of my mother and father, who raised seventeen children in a very small house on a farm. I thought about what happened in my classroom, when I was teaching, compared to what took place in my house growing up. My mother and father bonded with me and my siblings, showed appreciation for us, made us feel secure, provided guidance and structure, held high expectations for us, and interacted with us constantly. Could educators employ some of the same strategies and techniques in the school and classroom to create a more disciplined environment? I decided to use examples from my family to illustrate for educators how meeting the need for connection, reward, security, and support services would enhance discipline in their schools and classrooms.

The composition and function of a family mirror the com- position and function of the classroom, and the same needs exist within both. The same desires or urges are present in the family and the classroom because human needs are not situation-specific. Human beings have the same needs that must be addressed no matter where they are. Using this information, I developed a four-faceted model as a framework for meeting the needs of students with the goal of reducing discipline problems.

I wrote *RULES and CONSEQUENCES: One Major Reason Why They Don't Always Work and What Else Teachers Can Do* to provide a tool for teachers to reduce the amount of time they spend on discipline. Increased instructional time has a direct correlation to improved student achievement. When connection, reward, security, and support services are addressed, there is a positive impact on discipline. For educators to meet the needs of students, they must be able to understand what those needs are and how to satisfy them in the classroom.

Chapter 1

THE FAMILY AND THE CLASSROOM

A classroom is like a family. How many people are in your family? How old are they? How many boys and how many girls? What do they like to do? What are some items they like best and least? How do you reward them for good behavior? Do they get along with one another? How do you discipline them? These questions are likely to be asked of a parent, and teachers are often faced with the same questions concerning the students they teach. Hence, parents and teachers are routinely required to respond to similar issues in their respective roles.

Considering this, I thought about the composition of my family compared to the make up of a classroom and reflected on what happened in my family as compared to what takes place in the classroom. From this contemplation, I compiled a list of needs I found common among individuals in my family, other families, and the classroom.

My mother, father, sixteen siblings, and I constituted the makeup of my family when I was growing up. My siblings had different personalities, and my parents used a variety of techniques to teach us what we needed to know. Some of us would instantly do what was asked if my parents looked at us sternly. Others had to be scolded or spanked.

My family is now composed of my husband, three children, and myself. When my children were small, a removal of privileges that worked for one did not always work for the other two. I often had to find another approach, such as time out, for a different child.

Other families may consist of one parent, a mother or father, and the children or child. Grandparents or court-appointed guardians, in some cases, serve as the parents for the children in a family. Children in these families present the same dilemma apparent in my birth family and my current family. They all have different personalities and need to be treated accordingly.

Generally, teachers and students form the composition of the classroom. Sometimes, more than one teacher is placed in the classroom because of program requirements, such as a teacher assistant for kindergarten or to help profoundly handicapped students. Children in classrooms have different personalities and require a variety of techniques to effect changes in behavior and to boost achievement.

Parents, teachers, grandmothers, and legal guardians are adults. These adults are charged with the responsibility of teaching and guarding the well-being of the children in the home or school. Children in both situations are viewed as individuals who need specific emotional and psychological support to achieve and contribute to society. Therefore, what happens between adults and children in a family and a classroom will influence and help shape the behaviors of children.

What Happens in a Family and in a Classroom?

Reflecting on what happened in my birth family, I can remember my mother and father teaching me how to treat others and how to behave. Their instructions included be kind, tell the truth, don't tattle, don't fight, obey your teachers, don't talk back, work hard, and do your best.

My family played a major role in how I behave today and in my interaction with others. I taught my children some of the same principles and values. When I interact with my children, I see evidence in their lives of what I taught them when they were growing up. Recently, I was speaking unpleasantly about someone in the company of one of my children. She quickly reminded me that I told her it was wrong to gossip about others.

As a teacher and counselor, I have participated in numerous parent conferences where students were present. When the discussion focused on misbehavior, parents reminded their children how they were taught to behave. During one conference I attended, the parents scolded the student and revoked his driving privileges.

The family plays a major role in teaching children socially acceptable behaviors, principles, and values of our society. Families shape the opinions and beliefs many children hold about people, society, and themselves. In a family, children learn what acceptable and unacceptable behaviors are and what is expected of them.

A classroom is a place where students gather to learn from teachers. Individuals with different personalities populate these places of learning. The emphasis in a classroom setting is on such subjects as math, English, reading, or science. When I was a teacher, I frequently stopped instruction to address how students were behaving or interacting with me and how they were treating each other. These misbehaviors included talking excessively, arguing with each other, talking back to the teacher, using profanity, refusing to follow instructions, being rude, and calling each other names.

As a teacher, I found myself addressing some of the same behaviors in school with my students that I dealt with at home with my own children and that my parents handled with me and my siblings. My goals were to help students distinguish between appropriate and inappropriate behaviors. I also encouraged them to demonstrate common courtesies such as being polite and respecting other students.

Conduct students learn to view as suitable or improper in a classroom plays a role in how students behave. What happens between teachers and students in a classroom influences how students interact with others and the respect they have for themselves.

Four Common Needs in a Family and Classroom

Teaching is the primary focus of parents in families and of teachers in the classroom. Critiquing my personal family structure and my role as a classroom teacher helped me identify four needs of all students. When these needs are met, the probability of increased achievement is significantly enhanced, and incidents of misbehavior are reduced. The four needs are:

- Connections

- Reward

- Security

- Support services

The Four-Faceted Discipline Framework

My parents made a positive connection with us from the day we were born by comforting us when we cried as well as laughing and playing with us. These simple acts helped them build a positive relationship with us. When I became a parent, I provided my children with encouragement and nods of approval, and I comforted them when needed.

When it was time for rewards for hard work on the farm, my parents used such rewards as candy, sodas, and longer rest periods. My children were acknowledged for appropriate behavior and academic achievement with such activities as skating and playing at a park.

I grew up in a home where I knew my parents loved me. I recall my father coming in after a hard day's work on the farm, picking us up, and bouncing us on his knee while he counted from one to ten. He often affectionately referred to us as "swank-and-bank" while he gently plucked a kiss from our cheeks with his fingers. My mother made quilts to ensure we would be warm during the winter. My parents' obvious affection made me feel secure and safe. My children enjoyed playing games of Monopoly with the family, eating special meals of macaroni and cheese and roasted home-style pork, and getting a surprise from their father. These types of activities added to their feeling of security.

My parents set rules and consequences, expected us to finish chores, provided guidelines for behaviors, established procedures and routines, and required obedience from us. These obligatory acts supported us in our development and encouraged achievement. My children were also expected to follow the rules, do chores, adhere to timelines, stick to procedures or routines, and respect our authority.

I spent several years as a classroom teacher and learned a lot about what children require to help them reach their full potential. Observing children in the classroom of my colleagues has increased my understanding of what children need to achieve. From my experience in the classroom and my observations of other classrooms, I have concluded that children must receive similar interactions and treatment from adults in the classroom or school as I needed from my parents and my children wanted from us. I can only imagine that children in other family situations desire the same.

Children need to develop a positive relationship with their teachers, be recognized for their accomplishments or effort, feel secure in the classroom environment, and have the essential support to be successful. Based on the obvious need of children for connections, reward, security, and support services, I developed the Four-Faceted Discipline Framework using these four needs.

The next four chapters are devoted to discussing each of the four facets and will offer strategies to help teachers address them. When these needs are met, teachers can do more teaching and increase time on task which will result in higher achievement.

Chapter 2

CONNECTION

THE first day of school, Mrs. Coggins, an English teacher, introduced herself to her students and invited the students to do the same. The introductions included names and what they preferred to be called, what they wanted other students to know about them, and information about their families. Then Mrs. Coggins told the students she would prefer to call them Mr. or Miss so-and-so. She explained that this showed a level of respect for them as individuals and adults she was preparing for the world. The students did not like it initially but warmed to the idea after the first few days. Many of the students said that it made them feel like Mrs. Coggins respected and liked them.

Mrs. Coggins made a positive connection with students the first day of the class by doing this one simple thing. By referring to all students as Mr. or Miss, Mrs. Coggins showed that she had respect for all students without regard to race, ethnicity, academic levels, or socioeconomic status. Mrs. Coggins provided a model of how to treat others with deference.

This chapter is about connections. When a positive connection exists between teacher and student, academic achievement increases. For the purpose of this book, I will focus on positive connections. Smiles, a nod of approval, an encouraging act, or an acknowledgement are all examples of positive connections. Developing positive relationships strengthens the connection.

Developing Positive Relationships

A positive relationship is one where mutual respect and positive regard co-exist. Developing positive relationships between teachers and students requires making a connection. Reflecting on personal beliefs, assumptions, and perceptions, having a plan for getting acquainted with students, and providing ten "*Ships*" will help teachers make connections.

Beliefs, Assumptions, and Perceptions

What teachers believe about various ethnic groups will influence how they respond to the needs of students from those groups. Schools are now places of rich cultural diversity, and teachers must respond appropriately to encourage the involvement and academic success of all students. When teachers reflect on their beliefs, assumptions, and perceptions, they become conscious of how they react to students.

Teachers must critique the impact of their attitudes toward children who are socioeconomically and culturally different from them. This process enables teachers to uncover any negative feelings and assumptions they might have that inhibit them from building positive relationships with students.

Mrs. Farr is a telling example of how personal beliefs and perceptions influence behavior. Mrs. Farr is an English as a Second Language (ESL) teacher. As I observed her class one day, she informally surveyed the class on her teaching methods and interaction with students. She wanted to know if the instructional methods were adequate to aid the students in learning English. She also quizzed students about how well she interacted with them. All students commented positively on the value and merit of the instructional methods she employed. But Mrs. Farr was surprised by the responses of some students regarding her interaction with them. Some students voiced concerns that she showed favoritism toward one of the students. The students believed that she thought this student was smarter than other students in the class. Some of the students told her she called on this student more than them to answer questions. This same student was allowed to run most of her errands and help in the classroom.

At first, Mrs. Farr vehemently denied it and was offended by the students' comments. After a lengthy discussion with the students, Mrs. Farr reflected on their comments. She admitted that her behavior could have been interpreted by some students as showing favoritism. She certainly did not intend to send this message, and she was deeply disturbed. She questioned how she interacted with former students and their perception of her interaction. Now that Mrs. Farr is aware of these problematic interactions, she vows to critique her interactions carefully with students in the future.

Another way for teachers to examine beliefs, assumptions, and perceptions is to think about how these ideas were formed. Examining what we think of others and how we treat others because of their appearance, economic status, or race is often uncomfortable. But this is necessary if we want to develop positive relationships. It is an inescapable fact that the thoughts of most people are influenced by what they see and accept as real. Perception is so powerful that it will make you deny reality.

I thought about how I formed my beliefs, assumptions, and perceptions about people like me and different from me. When I was a teenager, I occasionally watched television on visits to my grandma's house. The roles that black performers played were starkly different than those of whites. In many cases, black people played the roles of cook, housekeeper, nanny, comedian, and field hand. White people snapped up the roles of a millionaire, banker, professional, artist, and business owner. As an adult, when I watch television, the roles whites and blacks play have not changed much from when I watched television at Grandma's.

When people mispronounce words or use the wrong verb tense, others may think they are unintelligent. I remember being in a store and overhearing a conversation between the salesman and a customer. The customer was trying to find out some information about an item. The customer used words like "*dat*" instead of "that" and "*fetch*" in place of "bring" and "*reck collec*" instead of "remember." The salesman had to ask the customer to repeat statements several times before he understood what the customer wanted. I wondered who this person was and where did he come from? I even thought, "Is he ignorant?"

People are often judged by their appearances. Some people assume when individuals have dreadlocks or spiked green hair that they are involved in illegal activity, use drugs, listen to hard rock or gangster rap, or dislike school. Some believe if people wear braces, collared shirts, and khaki pants, they like fine arts, smart, and are trustworthy.

People's perceptions of others' economic status often influence how they treat them. When I shop at high-end stores, clerks follow me around or tell me how expensive items are. I am not usually carrying Coach Purses or wearing Prada shoes. Customers who look wealthy are offered several items from which to choose and given more personalized attention. If individuals live in the housing projects, some may think they are less savvy and educated than those who live in upscale communities.

If classroom teachers hold negative perceptions of students because of their appearance, economic status, or race, their ability to be objective is questionable. If teachers think students from low-income homes cannot learn, they will provide them with less challenging work than students from affluent families. When grading tests requiring short answers and essays, teachers who hold low expectations for Black or Hispanic students may be more critical of their answers than they are of other students' answers. Teachers who think students with dreadlocks are drug dealers may be distant and less accommodating to such students than to those who are clean-shaven and have schoolboy haircuts.

Why would teachers behave this way? Is it possible that they hold toxic beliefs, assumptions, and perceptions that impact how they interact with students? All educators must be cognizant of their beliefs, assumptions, and perceptions they hold of students. How they view students will impact how they advise them. If they believe a student is incapable of learning because of his race or socioeconomic status, they will not encourage them to attend four- year colleges. They may primarily guide them toward work or the military after high school, even if students may be well suited to college. Thoughts about students will determine how they advise them.

The story of one student, La Diamond, comes to mind as a telling example of how perceptions impact recommendations. Years ago, I helped rising ninth-grade students select classes for the following year. La Diamond was assigned to me. I reviewed his academic records from sixth and seventh grades. He earned mostly *A*s and *B*s in all subjects, yet his teacher recommended him for lower-level classes. This sparked my interest and caused me to question why. Perhaps it was his standardized test scores. I looked at the scores in his folder. His test scores were all above average. Perplexed, I discussed the recommendations with his middle-school counselor. She provided a plausible explanation that the teacher was new and really had not had the opportunity to learn the strengths of her students. I found this explanation troublesome since the teacher had been there since August and this was March. After further discussion, the middle-school counselor and I agreed to help La Diamond select classes from among the college preparatory options.

Educators, like most people, are products of their environment and are influenced by the messages society communicates about different groups of students. Some teachers view students through stereotypical lenses contaminated with personal beliefs, assumptions, and perceptions. When teachers view students through contaminated lenses, they may communicate low expectations for certain students.

Getting Acquainted with Students

Bonding is an important element of a plan for developing positive relationships. Bonding is the act of developing a positive relationship between two or more individuals by performing specific acts. The behavior of my mother with a newborn offers one of the finest examples of bonding I know.

My mother gave birth to seventeen children. Fifteen of them were born at home with the assistance of a midwife. My grandmother insisted my mother stay in bed for days after giving birth. I remember when Stephanie, my sister, was born. Stephanie had the full attention of my mother. For several days after Stephanie was born, my mother stayed with her in her bedroom day and night. Imagine the bonding that occurred between my mother and Stephanie. I remember my mother breast-feeding Stephanie, like she did all her children. This added to the bonding experience. She learned a lot about Stephanie's temperament, behavior patterns, and personality. She sensed Stephanie's needs and responded appropriately. Stephanie learned quickly that my mother cared and was there to supply what she needed.

Bonding between teachers and students is needed to create a positive relationship. The method in which this is accomplished may vary. The key is effective non-verbal and verbal communication. Spending some time focusing on developing positive relationships at the beginning of the school year will produce a better classroom atmosphere.

The word "developing" is important because it suggests that a good relationship does not happen instantly or automatically but requires specific and conscious actions. My mother performed specific acts to develop a positive relationship with Stephanie. I offer a few of her techniques:

- *Pay Attention and Observe.* It is important that teachers observe students. Observations always yield valuable information. During their bonding time, my mother gained insight into Stephanie's needs. There is no magical formula for observing students. Each teacher will find what works best for him/her. Continuous observation is important.

- *Avoid Favoritism.* As my mother was observing us, we were observing her. We were watching to see how she treated each of us. We wanted to make sure she did not show favoritism. If we thought she did, we were quick to point this out to her (cautiously and respectfully, of course). I believe that most sibling rivalry is the direct result of parents playing favorites. I think this is true in the classroom as well. Student rivalry can be linked to teachers having favorites. The other students usually dislike the "teacher's pet."

- *Develop a Relationship with the Students' Families.* Making the first connection with the family before meeting the child in a classroom situation can help teachers forge a positive relationship with family members. Teachers can introduce themselves by writing a letter, calling, emailing, or making a home visit. The contact will provide family members an opportunity to ask questions and learn about the teacher's experience, education, and family.

- *Take a Personal Interest in Each Student.* My mother made every effort to provide for each of our needs. Since there were seventeen children, it was a challenge each day. Teachers sometimes have more than seventeen unique students in a classroom and providing for the needs of each will present some difficulties. When I was in the classroom, I would design individual lessons or utilize learning centers to ensure that I would have some time to spend with individual students. I also used cooperative learning groups, where a few students worked together on an assignment. That provided me with some flexible time to work with specific students.

- *Examine Personal Assumptions, Beliefs, and Perceptions.* Teachers should critically and honestly assess their beliefs about others and how their behavior reflects those beliefs. They may find some surprising things about how their behaviors have impacted the development of positive relationships.

Ten "Ships"

A ship is one of the oldest and most important means of exploration. Ships aided Columbus in discovering a new world. Magellan during his explorations proved that the Earth is round. People also were and are seeing new places because a ship can take them there. I sailed to the Grand Bahamas Islands and Mexico several times. My first trip provided me with an opportunity to see new kinds of flowers, interact with people of a different culture, and walk in an ocean of beautiful blue water. I explored these new places because a ship took me there. These experiences helped me gained a greater appreciation of the diversity that exists in the world.

Ships were and are vital to commerce and a growing economy. Ships have brought tea from China, gold from Mexico, oil from the Middle East, and diamonds from Africa. Throughout history, countries and individuals have become rich and powerful by using ships to move goods across the sea. Ships provided a means of helping many people improve the quality of their lives by selling or trading goods brought by ships. Ships were and are important to the prosperity and strength of a nation and the people who live there.

Because of ships, new relationships were formed, and old ones were strengthened. As demand for goods increased, ships became more important to merchants and their customers. As with many things, I imagine word spread about the goods ships were supplying and the positive impact this merchandise had on living conditions. Other people in neighboring lands probably wanted a piece of the action.

Just as countries and people used and are using ships to build strength, gain power, become prosperous, increase knowledge and forge new relationships, children need ships to help them become emotionally strong, powerfully confident, and academically rich. Ships that take people across the ocean and transport goods are made from wood, iron, or engineered material. Ships children need come from the human spirit. When these ships are provided to children, the relationship between student and teacher is enhanced.

I invite teachers to let these ships sail each time they have an opportunity to interact with children. I do not provide a definition of these ships because it is important that the captains of these ships maintain authenticity in the way they navigate them. Keep it honest, open, and frequent is my advice to teachers so that a meaningful relationship can be developed.

The ten "Ships" are:

Leadership

Membership

Sponsorship

Partnership

Fellowship

Guardianship

Mentorship

Censorship

Championship

Friendship

Chapter 3

REWARD

REWARD is the act of recognition and appreciation. Students must be provided opportunities to earn rewards. These opportunities should be varied and numerous enough so that earning a reward is possible for all students. Rewards can be tangible or intangible and span from simple to elaborate. They can be in the form of verbal praise, certificates of achievement, special time with the principal, gift certificates, or homework passes.

The relevance of rewards will impact the value students place on them. Presenting these rewards at Parent and Teacher Organization (PTO) meetings, during awards days, in class, or at banquets validates the work of students and enhances their self- esteem. The positive effects of receiving rewards are enhanced when the rewards are given immediately and/or on specific dates of which students are aware.

I learned that rewards could change how students feel about being in the classroom and encourage them to work hard. One method that I used as a teacher that was popular with students was called the starboard. I designed the board to recognize student achievement and effort. When students completed an assignment or project or put forth their best effort, I placed a star next to their names on a decorated bulletin board. When the students accumulated ten stars, they could visit the prize box.

The prize box was a shoebox that contained an assortment of items I collected from businesses in town, such as food coupons, candy, school supplies, art supplies, and toys. I gradually decreased the frequency of visits to the prize box to allow intrinsic motivation to develop. Over time, achieving academic success and having engaging work were enough to keep students motivated to put forth their best effort.

Another favorite with the students was sub days. The local Substation II donated several foot-long submarine sandwiches, cookies, and drinks each month to the class to celebrate their achievement. All students participated because each turned in completed homework, made progress in a specific subject, earned the highest grade on a test, finished a project, or spelled a list of words correctly.

Engaging Work

Providing engaging work designed around varied and innovative instructional strategies is one way to keep students inspired and make learning fascinating. Some examples of different strategies to grab and keep students' attention are: assigning projects to complete, arranging scavenger hunts, having students conducting research, encouraging students to visit local businesses, making scrapbooks, facilitating discussions, and organizing field trips.

Mrs. Steele, a sixth-grade teacher, takes her students to the State House to observe how lawmakers work together to enact laws. Students spend the two weeks after their field trips writing bills, debating them, and voting the bills into law. Mr. Rawls, an eighth-grade teacher, takes his students to a local farm to see cotton plants when he teaches about slavery. He then tells students to work in groups to write reports on the relationship between cotton and slavery. These are two cases where teachers utilized engaging strategies to hold the attention of students and add to the learning experience.

Another means of capturing student interest is to present lessons that hold some value for them using appealing and relevant instructional materials and supplies. Some examples of these include PowerPoint, art supplies, videos, smart boards, internet, real-life examples, and Games.

Mrs. Gibbs demonstrates how teachers can select materials that will encourage students to participate by gaining and maintaining their attention. Mrs. Gibbs, a fourth-grade teacher, instructs students in how to use PowerPoint. Students must create a PowerPoint presentation about themselves and present it to their classmates. Students in her class also produce Power- Point presentations about life at their school. Using a digital camera, students take pictures of people and activities at school. They then use the pictures to make a presentation they share with other classes. Students enjoy making these presentations, and they learn a lot about technology in the process. Having to give presentations to their schoolmates helps sharpen their public-speaking skills.

I learned the value of keeping the attention of students and using a variety of instructional techniques when I taught highly distractible students identified as having a learning disability. Marty, for example, did not know how to add. He liked jellybeans, so I decided to use jellybeans to help teach him addition. I would give him addition problems and jelly beans to use for counting. He was allowed to eat the jellybeans afterward. Knowing he could eat them after he successfully solved the addition problems held his interest and provided an incentive for him to learn how to do addition.

When students are occupied with completing projects, conducting research, or building models, it is less likely they will be involved in deviant behavior. The classroom can be an exciting place for students when they are enthralled in what they are doing. Students look forward to attending class and working with classmates. They share their knowledge and are eager to learn from others.

Chapter 4

SECURITY

MARY was a first- semester senior. She was overweight and often complained that she was teased by others. Her mother came to my office one day in late October to discuss Mary's graduation status. She asked if Mary had earned the required credits to graduate early. Mary felt she could not successfully deal with the teasing and put-downs from students any longer. Because Mary did not feel safe at school, she wanted to leave. Her mother supported her decision because she felt helpless to relieve the obvious emotional pain these insults were causing her daughter. We discussed counseling and a weight-loss program to help Mary.

After discussing Mary's case with the principal, he asked the staff to make recommendations on how to decrease teasing and name calling at the school. The staff recommended peer mediation program, discipline for offenders, an awareness campaign, and parent education. The principal accepted all recommendations and implemented them. It was too little too late for Mary. She completed all requirements for a high school diploma at the end of the semester and left school. Other students will benefit from the steps taken by the principal to ensure a safe school environment. They will likely feel comfortable and secure enough to graduate with their classmates.

Students need to feel safe in the classroom to perform at their optimum level of proficiency. By creating a safe and secure environment, teachers provide an atmosphere that is conducive to learning. Security is important to students, and it should be given high priority. Teachers should not tolerate teasing, bullying, or harassment of students. These types of behaviors create a hostile environment, making it difficult for students to concentrate on learning. To maintain a climate conducive to learning, teachers must decisively address any deviant behaviors immediately. Teachers can also set the tone for safety by having a clean, organized, and attractive classroom.

Classroom Environment

I decorated the nursery using shades of light blue for our sons, and yellow and pink for our daughter. I outfitted the crib with soft and fluffy linens and accessories. I placed a mobile over the crib that played nursery rhymes. The lights were another important ingredient in making the nursery comfortable and welcoming. I decided to use 25-watt light bulbs in each of the two lamps to make the room more peaceful. I turned down the lighting in the rest of our home and painted the walls in neutral and pastel colors before the children were born. We kept loud noises to a minimum, especially while the children were infants. It was essential to me that my children felt loved and secure, and I hoped the choice of colors, linens in the crib, the musical mobile, lights, and low noise created an inviting atmosphere of warmth and security.

An inviting classroom setting is the first step to developing a positive relationship with students. The appearance of a classroom can influence the relationship between a teacher and student. The atmosphere and attractiveness of a classroom communicate respect for the students. A neat, organized, and clean classroom will be welcoming to students. When students enter the classroom for the first time, they will sense the care devoted to making the classroom a pleasant place.

I visited a school in a different city several years ago, while I was still a teacher. While there, I observed teachers in some classrooms. One classroom made an everlasting impression on me because of its inviting atmosphere. It was the fourth-grade classroom of Mrs. Peterson. Mrs. Peterson's classroom had soft lighting, walls painted sky blue, bean bags and books placed around the room to create reading corners, the names of each student written in color on wooden planks and suspended from the ceiling, and walls decorated with student work and nature scenes. Mrs. Peterson had also installed plush carpet to bring additional warmth and comfort to the classroom. Mrs. Peterson's classroom made students feel important because of the time she spent in making her classroom a place that shouted, "Welcome!" I must admit, I was a little envious of her classroom.

Another factor in keeping the classroom safe is providing guidelines for behaviors. Posting these guidelines in a place of high visibility will help remind students what is expected of them. These guidelines could include bans on name calling, teasing, fighting, threatening other students, sexually harassing other students, and using profanity.

Students who choose to disregard these guidelines should receive referrals to an administrator for disciplinary action, phone calls to parents, in-school suspension, after-school detention, or revocation of parking privileges. These types of consequences are uncomfortable for students, prompting them to avoid repeating the same behavior.

By taking these steps, teachers demonstrate that they expect students to treat each other with respect. This establishes high expectations for student behavior, and high expectations are needed to maintain a secure environment.

High Expectations

When I was an elementary-school counselor, I worked with a fifth-grade student name Sally. Her parents and many of her teachers told Sally that she was hyperactive. Sally would blurt out answers, move around the class without permission, and talk excessively. There was no medical diagnosis to support the claims of her parents or teachers. I asked Sally whether she thought she was hyperactive, and she responded, "Well, if my parents think I am and some of my teachers say I am, then I guess I am." Sally conducted herself like others expected her to. Students live up or down to expectations. Sally's story demonstrates how attitudes or beliefs can influence behavior.

Students know what teachers expect from them by the behaviors they accept. Sally believed her teachers expected her to talk excessively and blurt out answers. Therefore, Sally acted accordingly. If her teachers had insisted Sally curtail her talking or raise her hand before answering a question, it is likely that Sally would have behaved differently. A cycle of unacceptable behavior and low teacher expectations exists when students are not corrected and are allowed to misbehave.

Robbie is another poignant example of what can happen when teachers communicate that they do not have high expectations. I met Robbie, a tenth grader, when he came to the school counseling office to speak with me. Robbie said he hated school and was upset with his teacher because he felt ignored and mistreated. He surmised that the teacher did not like him. Robbie compared how the teacher treated him with how he treated other students. The teacher would answer questions posed by other students and ignored Robbie's raised hand. Robbie thought the teacher did not think he was very smart. Robbie became discouraged and stopped trying. It is important that students think teachers have high expectations for them.

The story of another student, Sandy, provides another illustration of the importance of high expectations and acceptance. One of the rules in Sandy's fourth-grade classroom was, "Raise your hand before speaking." The consequences each time a student broke the rule progressed from a warning to a referral to the principal. The consequence for the second infraction was the loss of free time. The teacher warned Sandy four times before he took away Sandy's free time. Sandy protested, saying the teacher failed to take away his free time when he committed the second offense.

I wonder if Sandy would have called the action of the teacher into question if the teacher had removed his free time immediately after his failure to raise his hand before speaking the second time. It is critical that students know they will be held to high expectations and that nothing less will be accepted.

Chapter 5

SUPPORT SERVICES

SUPPORT services are a set of activities that facilitate appropriate behavior in the classroom. Class meetings, rules, consequences, class beliefs, class goals, routine, procedures, and class roles guide students' behavior as they interact with the teacher and each other. Teachers can use these activities to provide structure and boundaries and to enhance the learning environment.

Class Meetings

When I was growing up, my parents held meetings with us, especially when it was time to do farm chores like pick cotton, hoe cucumbers, or harvest tobacco. My father would assemble us around him to show us how to hoe around the cucumber plants without chopping them up or demonstrate how to remove a tobacco leaf from the tobacco stock. Sometimes we would gather in one room in the house to hear my parents talk about what growing up was like for them. They would tell us about having to walk to school and the kind of discipline they received from their parents. My father, especially, would slip in a few words of wisdom on how to achieve more than what he was able to accomplish in his life. He believed that education was the key to financial freedom and independence.

Many of our family meetings occurred during mealtimes. My husband and I held family meetings with our own children to address specific issues. As the head of the household, my husband facilitated the discussions. We held one such discussion when we contemplated moving to another city. My husband was offered a position as a principal, and it meant a slight pay increase. Our children objected strongly because they did not want to leave their school or friends. Since it was not a significant pay raise and the children were a few years from finishing high school, we decided to wait. Another time we held a family discussion when we needed to purchase a car. My husband and I wanted a van for its practicality and reasonable price. The kids preferred a sporty car. We decided to purchase the van. We valued the opinions of the children, but they did not always get what they wanted if it was not in the best interest of the entire family. At other times, we would discuss vacations, meals, clothes, and choosing friends. Sometimes we would share stories with them about how we grew up and how hard we worked for what we had accumulated. Often, we would use the family occasions to encourage our children to do their best and to instruct them on how to become better students and earn the respect of others.

During these gatherings, we learned a lot about our children, and they understood more about our thought processes. We came to understand and appreciate each other's differences and how our uniqueness added to the family. We used these family meeting times to express our opinions, protest, laugh, and reflect.

Classroom meetings can be held for the same reasons as family gatherings. They can be occasions to share ideas, inspire, share stories, make decisions, discuss issues, resolve problems, and have fun.

An environment where students are given an opportunity to share ideas and express feelings is important and can provide a sense of security. Classroom meetings provide opportunities for classmates to learn more about each other. Students will come to understand how individual differences make the classroom setting more interesting and how their uniqueness add to its diversity.

When my husband was an elementary school principal, he asked me to develop a program to help teachers create a safe classroom environment. I was a high school counselor at the time, but he felt since I had worked as an elementary counselor for many years, I understood the elementary setting. I had also developed a similar program when I worked as an elementary counselor for teachers to use at my school. I agreed to modify that program to fit the needs of his teachers and students.

Teachers at my husband's school wanted strategies to help them develop positive relationships with students and to help students develop positive relationships with each other. One of the major concerns was the amount of instructional time being consumed by teachers addressing interruptions, disrespectful behavior, and conflicts.

The school climate report showed teachers spending forty- five minutes to one hour daily addressing these problems. This, of course, was affecting the morale of teachers and other students in the classroom who were eager to learn. The school's discipline system of referring students to the principal, suspending students, or sending notes home to the parents obviously was not enough to deal effectively with these problems. Therefore, beyond maintaining and using the current system, my husband wanted to offer additional strategies to address student misbehavior.

The program I developed was called "Teachers as Mentors." Class meetings could provide an avenue for students and teachers to interact with each other in a family-type setting. In this situation, teachers could encourage and guide students by discussing issues, resolving conflicts, establishing and reviewing expectations, and talking about personal and school concerns.

When this type of support is offered, students respond positively. Darren is a case in point. Darren, a fifth-grade student at my husband's school, had a history of disruptive behaviors. He would threaten and yell at other students and often refused to complete written assignments. His behavior showed a remarkable improvement after several class meetings. During some of these meetings, Darren talked about how he felt when students teased him about mistakes he made when he read. Students stopped teasing him after they heard how much their laughter and name calling hurt him. Class meetings provided a safe place for Darren to express his feelings.

I designed the Teacher as Mentor program to help students address issues in a safe environment before these matters caused problems in the classroom or the school. Here is how the program worked. The faculty and staff generated a list of issues that caused classroom disruptions, conflicts between students, and conflicts between teachers and students. Students in each class also generated a prioritized list of issues. It was important for students to have input. Then the faculty and staff combined the student lists with theirs to generate one comprehensive list. The comprehensive list was prioritized by the faculty and staff, published, and posted.

The first fifteen minutes of each day was devoted to a discussion of one of the issues on the list. This was a time for building relationships, setting goals, and establishing behavioral expectations for the day. Students in all classrooms discussed the same problem. There were fifty issues on the list. Teachers discussed a different subject each day. Students could also share other concerns that could affect their behavior or academic performance for that day. Many times, students would talk about home issues or problems in the neighborhood.

Jamel, a sixth-grade student, offers a touching example of what students will share given the opportunity. Jamel lived in a neighborhood where gang activity was prevalent and where people sold drugs on the street corners. Jamel was offered drugs daily and was frightened to walk home from school because of the presence of gang members and drug dealers on his route home. Teachers were asked to allow students like Jamel to see the counselors if they felt students needed more help or guidance.

The last fifteen minutes of the day was devoted to "debriefing." This was another opportunity for students to talk about the day's activities, and it allowed teachers time to encourage and reward students. They also discussed expectations for the next day, so students would come mentally ready for work and appropriate behavior.

Teachers met each week by grade level to evaluate the program and make suggestions for improvement. The grade-level chair was asked to submit a written report to the principal. My husband received positive feedback about the effectiveness of the program from his teachers. Teachers indicated that fifteen minutes at the beginning and end of the day made a significant difference. Teachers were glad to have time to spend talking with students, and the students responded with a decrease in interruptions, disruptions, and conflicts. They were able to discuss issues openly in the classroom with their peers and teachers. By the end of the year, teacher morale had improved, and students were focused more on academics.

The Teacher as Mentor program is one way of conducting class meetings. Class meetings can be handled in several ways. Teachers must decide how they want to conduct class meetings that are appropriate for the students.

Organizing Class Meetings

Organizing class meetings requires planning and making important decisions. The most important decision is the frequency of class meetings. Class meetings can vary from daily to monthly. The frequency of meetings should be based on the social needs and developmental stage of students.

Consistency is the key to success. Canceling meetings repeatedly will give the impression that they are not a priority. Display a calendar of meeting dates and times. The calendar should include make-up dates for meetings missed due to emergencies.

The format of meetings is another critical decision to be made. Will it be a round-table discussion, or will students remain in their seats? Chairs arranged in a circle support and encourage interaction between students and the teacher. In addition, chairs organized in a circle allow the teacher to regularly survey the interaction between students to determine if intervention is needed. This type of arrangement makes the environment safe. Students who have experienced past conflict with each other should not be seated beside one another.

What will be the length of the class meetings? Establishing the length of time is important. Students should know when the meetings will start and when they will end. Setting a time limit on the meetings will encourage students to keep comments brief so all students who want to share will have time to do so. The length of the class meetings should be established at the first meeting and strictly adhered to.

A decision to determine if the meetings will be structured or unstructured must be made. Will there be an agenda? Will students be allowed to spontaneously bring up topics? Will the teacher decide on topics? Will students organize the meetings? Emotional maturity and age of the students are important considerations as to whether the meetings should be structured or unstructured.

Holding class meetings is one way of communicating care and concern for students. Class meetings encourage positive relationships by allowing time for students to connect with their teachers and their classmates. Class meetings validate and recognize the need of students to connect with others in a secure environment. Successful class meetings will depend on format, time, and the value placed on the meetings.

Goals

Setting goals is important to the success of students. Completing group projects, doing well on state tests, and completing all assigned work are a few examples of goals a class may try to reach. When students are working toward a goal, they are focused and make decisions to help them reach their goal. Goals that are reasonable and attainable keep students motivated. Too many or unreasonable goals can result in student apathy. Posting classroom goals is also important because they provide a visible reminder.

Class goals encourage collaboration. Collaboration can have a positive impact on relationships. Students hold each other accountable and provide support. A bond is likely to be created between students as they work together. They use each other's talents and gifts to complete assignments.

Providing an opportunity for students to have input when class goals are developed encourages support and cooperation. Students feel they have a personal stake and obligation to help manifest the goals when they help create them. Because of this allegiance, students often use peer pressure to encourage compliance.

A student by the name of Smith is an impressive example of what happens when peers apply pressure to do what is right. Smith's teacher shared this story at a departmental meeting to illustrate how students can work together to achieve a common goal. The teacher wanted to improve performance in a geometry class. The class decided that one-way students could earn better grades was to practice more at home. They set a goal of having each student complete and turn in all homework assignments for three consecutive weeks. The class would be rewarded with an A for a test grade that would be part of their final grade if they met this goal. Smith was known for procrastinating and handing in work late. Each day his classmates reminded him and encouraged him to complete his assignments. Students rotated calling Smith on the phone and urging him to come to school with the assigned work. At the end of three weeks, the class received the A.

To start the process of developing class goals, teachers should engage students in a discussion about their personal goals for the class. Discussing personal goals for the class will help students understand what you are trying to accomplish with them and why. Also, allow students to express their personal goals and how they feel you can work with them to accomplish their goals. If they are kindergarten through third-grade students, you may want to use pictures to help them understand their goals.

Generate a list of goals for the class. Write these goals on the board. Discuss and revise the list if needed. You may want to divide the goals into weekly, monthly, or yearly goals. For elementary students, you may only want to discuss daily goals. For middle-school students, you may want to discuss daily, weekly, and monthly goals. Yearly goals might be appropriate for high school students.

Devote some time to discussing behaviors and attitudes that will allow the class to accomplish each goal. Write them on the board. Also, you should discuss strategies to help maintain these behaviors and attitudes after developing the goals.

During my tenure as a teacher, I developed goals and posted them around my classroom. The goals were stated in simple language to avoid confusion and incorrect or personal interpretation. When I transitioned to the position of a guidance counselor, the goals for my students remained constant: 1) Do the best you can each day, 2) Ask for help when you need it, 3) Come prepared to work, and 4) Respect the rights of others.

Once you have established goals, you can help students write poems, create songs, or draw pictures about their goals. Daily use of this type of presentation is easy and will constantly reinforce your goals and help establish and maintain a classroom environment that is conducive to learning.

The goal sheet on the next page may be used to record personal behavioral goals and classroom behavioral goals. Students should be encouraged to paste this sheet inside their notebooks. Teachers should display the class goals in a prominent place in the classroom.

Goal Sheet

Personal Behavioral Goals

List two goals you want to accomplish in this class. Please list one behavioral goal and one academic goal.

_____

What do you need to do reach your goals?

_____

_____

Class Behavioral Goals

List three behavioral goals you want the class to reach this year.

_____

What does the class need to do to reach your goals?

_____

_____

Rules and Consequences

I support the use of rules and consequences when they are only one aspect of a discipline program. Because of the role rules and consequences can play in a well-developed, multifaceted discipline program, I have included a discussion about them in this book. Growing up with sixteen siblings, I witnessed my parents dole out consequences because rules were broken. Rules and consequences in my home served two purposes: 1) They helped us understand and adhere to the social and cultural values of the family, and 2) they made us aware of deviant behaviors. Knowing what was acceptable and unacceptable made excuses invalid.

Rules

My parents had three simple rules: obey your parents and elders, respect yourself and others, and do your best. Our elders included individuals who were older or in positions of authority. Adhering to rules was a means of showing respect. Appropriate responses such as "yes, ma'am" and "no, sir" were also signs of respect. Respect for ourselves was demonstrated by how we dressed, behaved, and spoke. The use of profanity and dishonesty were considered signs of disrespect. Half-heartedly completing chores was an unacceptable behavior to my parents. These three rules guided my behavior and influenced my interaction with others.

A few simple rules are adequate to guide the behavior of students. Rules for behavior in the classroom should be based on the class's beliefs and goals. Teachers and students can generate a list of a few simple rules. The rules should be posted in a prominent place. Posting the rules serves as a constant reminder to students of behavioral expectations. A few sample rules are: respect yourself and others, follow instructions, be honest, be courteous, respect your property and that of others, and come to school prepared to work.

Establishing a positive relationship with students diminishes deviant behavior and reduces the reliance on rules. The better the relationship between teachers and students, the less teachers will need to interrupt instruction to address misbehaviors.

Consequences

I learned a lot by observing my parents when they doled out consequences. I learned consequences could be given in many forms. Sometimes the consequences were having us redo a task. Other times we were required to apologize. Often the consequence was a conversation with my father that seemed to last for hours. Frequently my parents used corporal punishment. I remember the spankings most because we were made to select our own "switch." A switch is a branch from a bush or a limb from a tree. After we picked one, my parents decided if it was the right size and length. If my parents did not approve of the switch, we were sent back until we brought one they liked. I usually got sent back more than once because I would select skinny, short ones. For some strange reason, my parents preferred larger and longer switches.

I recall a time in the eighth grade when I was sent back for a different switch because the first one was too scrawny. My offense was that I had left the cotton field to visit my aunt without permission. My siblings did not realize I had left for a while. When a neighbor who had seen me walking down the road told my father, my father was none too happy. After scolding me for leaving the field without permission from my oldest sister, he sent me to the yard to get a switch. I remember surveying the limbs on the oak tree and plum trees. When I spotted one I thought would be acceptable, I broke it from the limb of the oak tree, removed the leaves, and presented it to my father. He glanced at it and ordered me to bring another one. The second switch was round and thicker, but still he sent me back for the third time. I figured I might as well give him the kind of switch he wanted and be done with the spanking. Besides, each time he made me return to the tree for another switch, he got angrier. I did not slip away from the field again after that day.

We were not always aware what type of consequences my parents would choose, but we knew without a doubt that consequences were unavoidable when we broke a rule. My parents' main goal was to send a message of consistency. They wanted us to understand that a consequence was forthcoming every time we ignored a rule.

Carrying out consequences in the classroom can present a number of challenges for teachers. The greatest challenge to administering consequences is to minimize the loss of instructional time. The number of students in a class can impact how much time it takes to mete out consequences. The larger the number, the more time it takes to appropriately address student misbehavior. Time on task is important due to high-stakes testing and the requirement to teach state-mandated standards. The teacher can confront this challenge by compiling a list of consequences that apply to different behaviors. Teachers can then generate a list of appropriate consequence to address the inappropriate conduct. Some examples of suitable consequences are a loss of free time, sitting alone during lunch, call to parents, removal from the class, loss of privileges, referral to the office, and detention.

Pointers Learned

The pointers below are ones I gleaned from my parents. These pointers helped me establish rules and mete out consequences in the classroom. Little did I know growing up that the example my parents set for establishing rules and dispensing consequences would have a significant impact on my professional life.

- *Provide Parameters.* This may come in the form of rules, behavioral cues, or belief statements.

- *Hold students accountable.* There should be appropriate consequences for deviant behavior.

- *Be Fair.* Consistently enforce the rules with all students.

- There is no room for partiality.

- *Allow consequences to be fluid.* The severity of the con- sequence should be in direct proportion to the behavior. The reoccurrence of an inappropriate behavior should also be considered when consequences are given.

Classroom Beliefs

Mr. Dunbar, a teacher that worked at my school where I was a counselor, believed all students could learn. He often made comments at faculty meetings such as all students may not learn at the same rate or proficiency, but all could learn given appropriate support and using relevant strategies. He would stay late at school creating lessons to reach students who were having trouble grasping a concept. He did such things as make PowerPoint presentations, plan field trips, design group activities, create colorful charts, and bring in experts in the field. All his students did not make As and Bs, but none failed his world history class. Mr. Dunbar was an example to his students of how a belief can influence actions.

Establishing classroom beliefs will help create a favorable classroom environment for learning and appropriate conduct. Students will be reminded of expectations. Class beliefs could serve as inspiration when students are having trouble. Short and concise beliefs are easier for students to remember. Displaying these beliefs in a prominent place will encourage regular review. I offer a few sample beliefs: learning is important, effort makes a difference, respect for yourself and others is essential, appropriate behavior fosters learning, and all students can learn.

Involving Parents

Once a teacher is confident students understand the rules, con- sequences, goals, and beliefs, I recommend hosting a meeting for parents. At the meeting, the teacher should explain how these classroom guidelines were formulated. The teacher can talk about the rationale for each and emphasize the importance of parents working closely with the teacher to maintain a cooperative learning environment.

Teachers can present copies of the rules, consequences, goals, and beliefs to parents at the meeting. Responsibilities of the teacher, student, and parents can be listed on the form. Include signature lines to verify students, parents, and teachers agree with the content of the form. Ask parents to sign one copy to remain with the teacher and keep one copy for their records. The teacher should send a copy home with students to parents unable to attend the meeting. If needed, teachers or a home- school worker can make a home visit to answer questions for these parents. The teachers can also contact these parents by telephone to answer questions and to provide explanations. Offer incentives to students for returning a copy signed by the parents.

The sample form below provides a place for teachers to write rules, consequences, goals, and beliefs. Responsibilities of students, parents, and teachers are included as well as signature lines. The teacher should write the rules, consequences, goals, and beliefs before the form is distributed to students and parents.

Sample Form

Student's Name: _____

School: _____

Grade: _____

Teacher: _____

Subject: _____ Date: _____

Class Rules:

1. _____

2. _____

3. _____

Consequences:

1. _____

2. _____

3. _____

Goals:

1. _____

2. _____

3. _____

Beliefs:

1. _____

2. _____

3. _____

Responsibilities

Responsibilities of the Teacher

- Inform students of the agreement.

- Answer questions about the agreement.

- Discuss the agreement in detail with the students.

- Monitor students' adherence to the agreement.

- Provide appropriate feedback to students and parents.

Responsibilities of the Student

- Do all that is outlined on this form.

- Provide feedback to the teacher.

Responsibilities of the Parents

- Encourage students to do all that is outlined in the agreement.

- Engage students in conversation about their daily experience.

- Familiarize themselves with the agreement.

My signature on this form confirms:

- I agree to follow all rules.

- I understand and agree with all the consequences.

- I agree with the class goals.

- I agree with the class beliefs.

- I agree with my responsibilities.

Student's Signature: _____ Date: _____

Teacher's Signature: _____ Date: _____

Parent's Signature: _____ Date: _____

Principal's Signature: _____ Date: _____

Routines

My parents had an established routine for us, especially in the summer. They awakened us at five each morning, and we dressed in our farming gear: old and worn shirts, pants, skirts, shoes, and hats. We ate breakfast, and by six, we were ready for work on the farm. My parents believed in the concept of "The early bird gets the worm." These routines provided structure for me. I knew what to expect and I was not confused about what my parents wanted me to do.

Establishing routines for students in the classroom provides structure and consistency and lessens confusion. Students will know when to turn in finished work, when they can go to the bathroom, and when they can eat. Questions about what to do are eliminated when routines are established early.

Misguided behaviors caused by misinformation can result in conflict between the teacher and students. Routines reduce speculations or assumptions, thereby decreasing negative inter- actions between the teacher and student. Teachers and students enjoy a relationship that is more whole-some when routines are established.

When I taught students identified as needing special education, routines were essential to the smooth operation of my classroom. Many of these students became disoriented or uncooperative without established routines. Students knew we would have a break at 10:00 a.m., lunch at noon, and recess at 1:00 p.m. They had library time on Wednesdays at 9:00 a.m., and they visited with the music teacher on Thursdays at 11:00 a.m. Any deviation from the established routine required a full explanation ahead of time and several reminders. Routine provided structure and consistency for my students. They knew what to expect and what they needed to do to meet the expectations. This reduced conflict between my students and me.

Procedures

My parents also had procedures in place. We had no running water. The pump was located outside. We pumped water into pans or pots and brought the water inside. The water was poured into two different foot tubs and mixed with hot water for bathing. A foot tub is a round, heavy aluminum container that is a foot tall. The size and the height kept us from spilling water on the floor when we bathed. We took turns bathing in the foot tubs. The oldest girl and boy supervised and helped the younger children bathe.

When we finished bathing, we got dressed and got our breakfast. I can imagine the chaos in the absence of these steps. When the pump did not work, my parents had a backup plan: going to get water from my grandmother, who lived less than a quarter mile away.

Instituting procedures in the classroom will reduce confusion. Students will know how to turn in assignments, what to do when they want to go to the bathroom, and how they can eat in the classroom. Procedures provide step-by-step instructions for students. Alternative procedures should also be considered in the event it becomes impossible to follow normal procedures. Students will need to know how to respond when procedural changes are necessary. Procedures should be reviewed with students regularly and practiced daily. Teachers may want to establish procedures for: bathroom breaks, transitioning from one activity to the next, going to the cafeteria, turning in work, moving from class to class, putting materials away, going to a locker, dressing for physical education, responding when there is a fire drill, and keeping notes.

One teacher, Mr. Clear, had an established procedure for most events or tasks that occurred in his class. Immediately upon entering the class, the students were required to place their book bags on the top of their desks, take out their books, paper, pencil, assignments, and place them in their cubbies or desks. Once they were emptied, book bags were always placed on the wall hangers designated for each student. At the completion of each assignment, one student would collect the assignments and give them to Mr. Clear. Students were lined up, girls first, to walk to the cafeteria for lunch. At the end of the day, students retrieved their book bags, packed everything they wanted to take home, and waited quietly. This happened five minutes before the bell sounded. Mr. Clear's classroom was rarely disorderly, and his students were usually well behaved.

Class Roles

When I was growing up, the roles of children and the roles of teachers were clear. The teachers set clear boundaries for children, and the children were required to operate within those boundaries with the full support of parents. Teachers were regarded as the final authority. Children honored teachers and complied with most guidelines set by them. My parents revered teachers. They gave them the right to do whatever they deemed appropriate if I talked back or refused to follow directions.

In recent years, attitudes about roles have changed. Teachers are no longer viewed as the final authority. The authority of the teacher is under siege. Students are allowed, and sometimes encouraged, to confront and question the actions of teachers. A large percentage of teachers' time is spent justifying their actions to parents rather than on instruction.

This adversarial situation can erode the relationship between the teacher and student. Clarifying roles of teachers and students can stabilize the erosion. Parents have the luxury of clarifying roles over time as circumstances and situations dictate. Teachers do not have this advantage. The demands of meeting curriculum standards limit the time of teachers. In the face of changing attitudes about roles, teachers are put in positions where they must waste time to communicate their positions of authority and demonstrate how this authority functions in the classroom.

I conducted an informal survey of a group of high school teachers. The survey provided clues to what teachers think about the roles of students and teachers. The survey asked: 1) What is the role of the teacher? and 2) What is the role of the student? As expected, answers varied. The consensus was that the role of the teacher is to teach and enforce rules. The role of the student is to learn and obey the rules.

Here are some of the most interesting responses concerning the role of the teacher:

- To show that learning is lifelong. No one is ever through learning.

- The role of the teacher is to make sure there is a safe and loving learning environment for all students and visitors, to be knowledgeable of subject matter and prepared to teach with a variety of styles, and to encourage students to live properly, respecting all peoples whom they might encounter during school and outside of school.

- Guide, support, teach, inspire, listen, and believe.

- Role of a teacher: guide, direct, love, inspire, counsel, facilitate learning, provide food for thought, remember everyone messes up and that we teach CHILDREN!

- The role of a teacher is to guide the students in a pathway that will help the student cope with the obstacles that will confront them in their life.

- To facilitate the learning of students to help them prepare for future endeavors in life beyond high school (college/workplace/military).

- Relationship builder.

- Someone who must be good at their craft, enjoys teaching it, and adores relationships with teens to have success in preparing the student for life.

- We are supposed to excite the student into wanting more than just what is required. We are supposed to get them excited about their life and what they will do with it once they leave us. I know that a lot of the information we give to students does tend to look like "trivial pursuit" knowledge, but I think I am helping prepare the student for the role of "contributing" adult. If we can connect the information to the real world, we are successful, and so are they!

- Know and understand the needs and abilities of students.

- To provide instruction that is both challenging and interesting.

- To motivate, enthuse, and care about the student.

- Role model, guide, listener, craftsman, imparter of knowledge/skill, demonstrator, dependable, stable adult, and not a quitter (don't give up on the kids).

Some of the fascinating replies regarding the role of students were:

- To respect all people, follow all rules; be respectful of people's property, feelings, opinions, and customs. Students are to listen to adults and trust in what they are teaching them in the educational environment. Lastly, they are to learn at every opportunity.

- The role of a student is to face each task with the goal of trying his or her best and using all his or her potential to the fullest.

- Listen, learn, question (in a polite manner), be open to new ideas, remember everyone messes up, admit mistakes, and attend school.

- The role of the student is to learn not only the academics but also to learn to listen to the advice given to him/her by his teachers. The students must realize that the road to success is paved with hard work, patience, and perseverance.

- To work hard to pursue their education to reach their full potential and achieve success in the future.

- The role of students is to develop themselves to be the best that they can be to themselves and to others of the world.

- Try, improve, learn, listen, have an open mind, try again, go the extra mile, inspire, believe.

- Students are here to learn how the world looks outside of their bubble. Students are here to learn as much as they can to reach their goals for adulthood, whether those goals are to become doctors, mechanics, or parents. Students are here to get all they can to fit into the adult role appropriately and be able to survive. Many times, I think that if kids can survive public education and high school, they can survive anything. Unfortunately, the kids often don't see that until it is too late to be all they could have become.

- Come to class prepared to have their minds "filled." By that, I mean by respectfully listening and learning.

- Someone who takes ownership of his education.

Clarifying Class Roles

Clarifying roles of teachers and students is helpful. Knowing what the teacher expects of students can eliminate questions about position and authority. Clarifying roles is most beneficial if done at the beginning of the school year.

Teachers can clearly articulate their role and the role of students. This can be completed within one hour on the first day of school. It is important that the teacher allow time for questions from students. The following suggestions have worked well for other teachers.

1. Explain why clarifying roles of the teacher and student is helpful. The most powerful and useful reason is so the students will know what is expected of them.

2. Develop a list of student roles. Keeping the list to a maximum of five concise entries facilitates better understanding and lessens confusion.

3. Articulate beliefs about the roles of the teacher and student.

Social Adjustment

The last suggestion for support services is the importance of teaching social norms such as acceptable voice tone, appropriate greetings, and good communication skills. Many students in the public-school system do not understand the norms governing the social environment of the school. Because the school norms are derived from middle-class practices, some students from low socioeconomic backgrounds struggle behaviorally in this system. The students find it difficult to integrate because their social experience is different. This can produce fear, anxiety, and frustration.

Knowing and understanding the standards of behavior will enhance the students' ability to matriculate successfully in the school environment. If schools can only embrace one set of social norms, they have an inherent responsibility to teach the customs of the one they embrace. I spent many years working with students from various social environments. Many students that grow up in homes with parents of significant financial means do well in the public-school system. There could be many reasons for this, but I have concluded one reason is that the social norms of these homes mirror the social standards found in the school. Some of these standards are organizational skills, use of proper English, listening skills, and voice tone and pitch. Students who did not grow up in homes with the same norms find it more difficult to achieve in school. Helping these students understand the social norms of the school system will reduce their frustration. This will enable them to operate with a sense of security and confidence.

The number of ninth -and -tenth grade students at my school from low socioeconomic communities referred for discipline has increased over the past three years. The assistant principals report that most of the referrals are linked to disruptive or disrespectful behavior or disrespect toward adults and students. Teachers attribute many of these behaviors to community differences. Students often validate their behavior by pointing to the fact that their parents and people in their community accept the behavior.

When the assistant principals demand students behave according to norms different from their own, students rebel. Some students go so far as to label them as racist and uncaring. This opposition could be linked to the students' loyalty to their community and their beliefs that to behave in any other manner makes them traitors. Other students may respond in a disruptive or disrespectful manner because they are not skilled in the use of appropriate and acceptable responses in the school environment. The assistant principals report that consequences such as detention, in-school suspension, out-of-school suspension, and work detail have been minimally effective in reducing referrals for many of these students.

My school was forced to look for other ways of reducing these types of behaviors so the learning environment in the classroom would cease to be compromised. If any of these behaviors are associated with different cultural norms, and the students need to acquire alternative responses, what is the solution?

According to my observation and comments made by teachers, counselors, and administrators that I surveyed, students would get- along better with others, reduce referrals, and increase academic achievement if they become skilled at the following:

- Appropriate voice tone and pitch

- Organizational skills

- Dining etiquette

- Resolution of conflicts with adults and peers

- Entering and leaving a classroom properly

- Acceptable eye contact

- Using proper English vs. slang

- Understanding personal space

- Appropriate joking, jesting, and laughing

- Listening skills

- Handling embarrassing situations

- Avoiding discussions that could result in hurt feelings

- Making introductions

- Taking turns

I identified activities to teach these skills to students who had a history of disruptive behaviors and who were disrespectful to teachers. Case in point was a student name William. He lived in a community where profanity was an acceptable means of expressing anger with peers and adults. William was repeatedly referred to the assistant principal for using profanity with teachers. Several of these referrals resulted in a suspension. I used role-playing and an activity called "how to read people like a book" to help William understand why profanity is not appropriate or acceptable language in the school environment. I also worked with him on alternative ways to express his anger or dissatisfaction. He agreed to talk to his friends or me before addressing his teachers when he was upset. William reduced the number of referrals for using profanity when talking with his teachers.

Acquiring these skills will help students as they respond to individuals in an environment different from their own. The more students acquiesce to the social expectations of the school environment, the more successful they are at school. If educators want students to exhibit desirable behaviors, they must be willing to teach the skills needed. They also should be agreeable to developing effective methods to encourage students to learn skills that would help them become more successful in the school environment. Just as parents teach children what they want them to know, the school must do the same.

The expectations of a particular social environment are in force all the time, whether one understands or notices. The use of proper English is expected. If students use the wrong verb tense or pronouns incorrectly, they are mocked. A student is expected to know and follow the rules of etiquette when dining. Students are expected to keep the area around their desks neat and orderly. Failure to do so may be mistaken for rebellion. Students who do not follow directions or have difficulty with the process are often labeled as illiterate or disabled. Students who use slang when greeting others or talk loudly might be considered socially inept. If students' body language and tone of voice communicate aggressiveness or anger, others will avoid them. If students want to be successful in the school environment, they must know, understand, and meet expectations of the school setting.

Teaching students social norms will help them respond appropriately to social situations that confront them in school. Teachers, counselors, and administrators will find many activities in etiquette books that are helpful in teaching these norms as well as commercially printed materials and information posted on the Internet.

Students need to learn and adhere to specific norms to facilitate their success in the school environment. I encourage all educators to consider using activities to teach students how to be socially successful in the school environment. The more socially astute students become, the better they will feel about being in the school environment, and the more respectfully they will be treated by others. It has been my experience that others tend to hold higher expectations for individuals who ascribe to norms of the social environment.

Conclusion

Students need connection, reward, security, and support services. When these needs are addressed, the number of discipline problems is reduced. Developing a positive relationship with students, providing a safe and secure environment, rewarding students appropriately, and offering appropriate services can satisfy the need for connection, reward, security, and support services.

When educators use the strategies discussed in *Rules and Consequences: Why They Don't Always Work and What Else Teachers Can Do*, student behavior will improve. Improved student behavior will have a positive effect on the classroom. Teachers will be free to focus on academics because they will spend less time addressing misbehavior of students. Students will feel educators care for them, and they will respond with mutual respect.

Also by Regenia Mitchum Rawlinson

A Mind Shaped by Poverty: Ten Things Educators Should Know

A Mind Shaped by Poverty: Hidden Reasons for Poverty We Don't Talk About

From Discipline to Responsibility: Principles for Raising Children Today

Helping Students Overcome Roadblocks to Achievement

I Send My Child to School, What More Do You Want?

I Teach My Heart Out Every Day, What More Do You Want from Me?

School Counselors Helping Students Succeed: A Guide to Developing a Comprehensive School Counseling Program in Your School

About the Author

Regenia Mitchum Rawlinson has been an educator for over thirty years. She has served as a special education teacher, elementary school counselor, high school counselor, career development facilitator, and high school director of guidance.

Rawlinson has been sharing her insights about discipline with other educators since 1997. She is a local, state, and national presenter.

She lives in South Carolina with her husband, David. They are the proud parents of three adult children.